Water

Susan Canizares • Pamela Chanko

Scholastic Inc.
New York • Toronto • London • Auckland • Sydney

Acknowledgments

Science Consultants: Patrick R. Thomas, Ph.D., Bronx Zoo/Wildlife Conservation Park; Glenn Phillips, The New York Botanical Garden; **Literacy Specialist:** Maria Utefsky, Reading Recovery Coordinator, District 2, New York City

Design: MKR Design, Inc.

Photo Research: Barbara Scott

Endnotes: Susan Russell

―――――――――――

Photographs: Cover & pg. 1: Kim Taylor/Bruce Coleman, Inc.; p. 2: T. Eggers/ The Stock Market; p. 3: SuperStock; pp. 4-5: Zefa-Rainman/The Stock Market; pp. 5 (inset), 6 & 7: Barbara Gerlach/DRK Photo; p. 7 (inset): SuperStock; pp. 8-9: Robert Isear/Photo Researchers, Inc.; p. 9 (inset): Gabe Palmer/Mug Shots/The Stock Market; pp. 10-11: Charles Krebs/The Stock Market; pp. 11 (inset) &12: David Stoecklein/The Stock Market.

Library of Congress Cataloging-in-Publication Data
Canizares, Susan, 1960-
Water / Susan Canizares, Pamela Chanko.
p. cm. -- (Science emergent readers)
"Scholastic early childhood."
Includes index.
Summary: Photographs and simple text describe some of the many liquid and frozen solid forms of water, such as rain, tap water, frost, ricers, and icebergs.
ISBN 0-590-10727-5 (pbk.: alk. paper)
1. Water--Juvenile literature. [1. Water.]
I. Chanko, Pamela, 1968-. II. Title. III. Series.
GB662.3.C36 1998
553.7--dc21   97-34215
                                                                      CIP AC

8   9   10   03   02   01   00   99

Water is everywhere.

A river is water.

This is too.

Rain is water.

This is too.

Frost is water.

This is too.

Snow is water.

This is too.

Ice is water.

This is too.

Is this water?

Water

Water indeed is everywhere. Water surrounds us. Earth is called the "blue planet" because more than three-quarters of the earth's surface is covered with water. Our bodies are made up of over three-quarters water. Plants, animals, and people wouldn't be able to live without water to drink. Water is one of the most important elements. Without it, there would be no life on our planet.

Water comes in many forms. The tiny, tiny molecules that make up every drop of water are in constant motion, even when the water looks very still. These molecules stay together as the liquid that we think of as water. But because they're moving all the time, water doesn't keep a shape of its own; it fills whatever container it's in. Heat makes the molecules move faster. At the surface, they break away from the other molecules and rise into the air as water vapor. This is another form of water, and we call this process evaporation.

When water is in its vapor form it rises higher in the atmosphere, where there is less heat. Here the vapor cools and condenses, and the tiny drops stick together to form bigger droplets that become clouds. Mist and fog are like clouds on the ground. They are formed when the water vapor is cooled by the surface underneath. When the conditions are right, these little drops condense more, get heavy, and fall from the clouds as rain. The rain drains into little streams that flow into rivers, and the rivers eventually flow to the sea, making the great water cycle that nourishes our planet.

Dew, another form of water, forms when the cooled air reaches a point at which it can hold no more water. This is known as the "dew point." Then water droplets form from the vapor settling on grass, leaves, or even the glass of cold soda you're drinking. Sometimes at night, when the air outside quickly cools down to below the freezing point, 32 degrees Farenheit, the water droplets turn into tiny ice crystals. In the morning, we see everything covered with sparkling frost.

Snow is another form that water can take. If the water that evaporates and rises up into the atmosphere reaches air that is below the freezing point, snow can form. The tiny droplets condense and form little ice crystals. Many of these tiny crystals stick together and form small six-sided flakes we can see. These are called snowflakes. When they are heavy enough to fall, the snowflakes sometimes fall through warm air that melts them and turns them into rain. But when they fall through cold air, we see snow on the ground.

The largest amount of water on the earth is in the oceans. This is salt water and we can't drink it. But when water evaporates from the oceans and rises to form clouds, the salt is left behind. The rain that comes down from the clouds is fresh water. It is the water we can drink. This is the water that fills our streams, rivers, lakes, and reservoirs. We also use our lakes and rivers for recreation. We fish, swim, and go boating in the summer. When the winter comes, the ponds and lakes can freeze. If the weather stays very cold, the ice becomes thick, thick enough to skate on! How else do we use ice every day?